AWESOME FORCES OF NATURE

RAGING FLOODS

Revised and Updated

Louise and Richard Spilsbury

Heinemann
LIBRARY

Chicago, Illinois

www.heinemannraintree.com

Visit our website to find out more information about Heinemann-Raintree books.

To order:

☎ Phone 888-454-2279

▣ Visit www.heinemannraintree.com to browse our catalog and order online.

Edited by Megan Cotugno, Abby Colich, and Andrew Farrow
Designed by Richard Parker
Original illustrations © Capstone Global Library 2004
Illustrated by Geoff Ward
Picture research by Hannah Taylor
Production by Alison Parsons
Originated by Capstone Global Library, Ltd.
Printed and bound in China by Leo Paper Products, Ltd.

13 12 11 10
10 9 8 7 6 5 4 3 2

Library of Congress Cataloging-in-Publication Data

Spilsbury, Louise.
  Raging floods / Louise and Richard Spilsbury.
    p. cm. -- (Awesome forces of nature)
  Includes bibliographical references and index.
  ISBN 978-1-4329-3782-9 (hc) -- ISBN 978-1-4329-3789-8 (pb) 1. Floods--Juvenile literature. I. Spilsbury, Richard. II. Title.
  GB1399.S65 2010
  363.34'93--dc22
                          2009037562

Acknowledgments

We would like to thank the following for permission to reproduce photographs: Art Directors & TRIP: **8** (M. Barlow); Capstone Publishers: **24** (Karon Dubke); Corbis: **14** (Bisson Bernhard), **19** (Gideon Mendel), **23** (Wolfgang Kaehler); Getty Images: **7** (AFP Photo/Rob Elliott), **27** (AFP/STR); Naturepl: **9** (Grant McDowell); Press Association: **5** (AP Photo/Karel Prinsloo), **11** (AP Photo/David Zalubowski), **12** (AP Photo/Jeff Pruyne), **15** (AP Photo/J. Pat Carter), **26** (AP Photo/Powel Rahman); Rex Features: **4** (Newspix/N. Edwards), **10**, **13** (Sipa Press), **16** (Sipa Press), **17** (Sipa Press), **18** (Sipa Press), **28** (Sipa Press); Science Photo Library: **20** (Geoeye); Shutterstock: **21** (Guy Erwood); Still Pictures: **18**, **22** (David Hoffman), **25** (Nigel Dickenson).

Cover photograph of a flood in Xiqiaoshan, China reproduced with permission of Rex Features (Sipa Press).

We would like to thank Dr. Ramesh Srivastava for his invaluable help in the preparation of this book.

Every effort has been made to contact copyright holders of any material reproduced in this book. Any omissions will be rectified in subsequent printings if notice is given to the publisher.

All the Internet addresses (URLs) given in this book were valid at the time of going to press. However, due to the dynamic nature of the Internet, some addresses may have changed, or sites may have changed or ceased to exist since publication. While the author and publishers regret any inconvenience this may cause readers, no responsibility for any such changes can be accepted by either the author or the publishers.

Contents

Any words appearing in the text in bold, **like this**, are explained in the glossary.

What Is a Flood?

A flood is when a normally dry area of land is covered by water. Floods are one of the most common natural disasters in the world. Floods can affect many different types of land, but occur most often in places where flat, low-lying land meets rivers or seas. When sea or river levels rise, water spills out onto the land.

Important water

Water is vital for living things. Humans drink water, wash in it, and use it for cooking. The plants and animals we eat also need water to survive. Yet, water can be very dangerous and damaging to people during a flood, especially if the flood comes without warning.

This Australian highway was overcome by flood waters in 2009.

The power of floods

When water rushes through a town, it can damage buildings and bury houses under mud. It may drown people if they cannot get away in time. Even after the water finally drains away, there are still problems. In China in 1931, as many as 3.7 million people starved after a flood ruined their **crops**.

In Mozambique in 2001, many people had to wait a long time before being rescued. Water covered so many roads and bridges that rescue workers were unable to reach the flooded villages.

FLOOD FACTS

1. After fires, floods are the most common of all natural disasters.

2. Many people who die in floods are in vehicles. They make the mistake of trying to drive through flood water.

3. Rushing water only 12 centimeters (5 inches) deep can knock down a person. That much water would only cover an adult's ankles!

What Causes a Flood?

Water falls from the air onto land as rain or snow. Then it drains into rivers and streams and eventually ends up in the ocean. Finally, the water **evaporates** from the ocean back into the air. This is called the water cycle. If lots of water falls at once, it cannot all drain away immediately, so some stays on the surface of the land for a short time. This small amount of flooding is normal. Bad floods happen when very large amounts of water arrive on land in a short space of time.

How does the water cycle work?

Most water that falls on land either drains into the soil as **groundwater**, collects in lakes and **reservoirs**, or forms ice at the **poles**. Living things use some of this stored water. The rest of the water that falls on land drains into rivers that flow into the oceans. Heat from the sun evaporates water from ocean surfaces. This means it turns liquid water into a gas or vapor in the air. When water vapor cools again, it condenses—it changes back from vapor to liquid water. Droplets of the liquid water gather as clouds in the sky. The water then falls to Earth as rain, snow, or hail.

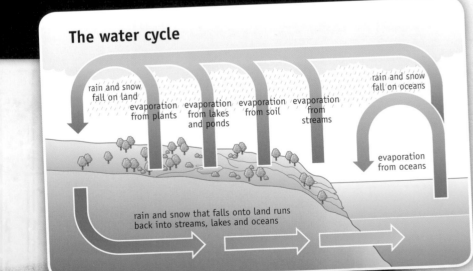

The water cycle

rain and snow fall on land

rain and snow fall on oceans

evaporation from plants

evaporation from lakes and ponds

evaporation from soil

evaporation from streams

evaporation from oceans

rain and snow that falls onto land runs back into streams, lakes and oceans

When do floods happen?

In **temperate** parts of the world, such as the United Kingdom, flooding happens most often in the spring and winter. These seasons are colder and wetter than summer and autumn. Large amounts of water arrive on land during heavy spring rains, which sometimes last for days or weeks. Water also collects on land in spring when large amounts of snow or ice that built up over winter begin to melt.

In **tropical** countries, such as Kenya, it is warm all year round. Most of the year's rainfall comes in one short, very wet season. This is called the **monsoon**. There are often floods during monsoons. Floods can also come after sudden heavy rainstorms or when large waves of seawater caused by earthquakes, hurricanes, or typhoons hit land. Seawater floods can happen at any time on low-lying coastal land that is near **sea level**.

Rains from a monsoon caused this flood in New Delhi, India, in 2003.

Making matters worse

Some natural conditions make flooding more likely. If soil is frozen or waterlogged (full of **groundwater**), water that falls onto it cannot drain away. It then stays on top of the land and builds up until it causes floods.

People also make things worse. They build **dams** and **reservoirs** to store water but these occasionally break or overflow, releasing tons of water all at once. When people cut down trees for firewood or for building with, wind blows away the top layer of soil that normally holds water. Without this **topsoil**, rainwater collects on the surface of the land. Also, in cities and towns, large areas of concrete around buildings and tarmac on roads stop water soaking into the soil. Drains may not be big enough to take away the water quickly, so it stays on the surface.

In China, large areas of land have little or no topsoil because of flooding. Without topsoil, few plants can grow.

Can floods be a good thing?

Some areas flood regularly. Low-lying areas that are usually affected by river flooding are called **floodplains**. The floodplains and **deltas** of big rivers such as the Nile in Egypt or the Mississippi often flood during heavy rain.

In spite of the threat of floods, floodplains and deltas can be good places for people to live. After floods, **nutrients** in the water soak into land making it **fertile** there. Some **crops**, such as rice, grow best in waterlogged soil.

Land that will flood is cheap to buy and is fertile. This is why lots of people live on or near floodplains, despite the risks.

What is a delta?

A river moves more slowly as it reaches an ocean. Small pieces of soil it is carrying drop to the river bottom forming a triangular area of land near the mouth of the river. This is called a delta.

9

What Are Flash Floods?

Flash floods happen very suddenly—in a flash! Flash floods can happen with little or no warning and they can become extremely dangerous within a very short time.

Flash floods are usually caused by sudden heavy storms, where a huge amount of rain falls in a short time. When the rain collects in a stream or river, it turns these gentle waterways into raging torrents. Flash floods are particularly dangerous because people don't have time to get out of the way.

> " *It's difficult to judge the depth, speed, and power of flood waters; in an instant, you can be swept into a drainage system or your car floated off a road or bridge.*
>
> —Rocky Lopes, Disaster Services worker for the Red Cross "

Flash flood water moves very quickly, destroying buildings, pulling up trees and rolling over cars in its path.

Fort Collins, 1997

On the evening of July 28, 1997, the people of Fort Collins, Colorado, were sleeping peacefully. They were unaware of the disaster that was about to happen. It had been raining since midday and the water had been collecting behind a railway **embankment**. Suddenly, at 11 p.m., a wall of water two stories high crashed through the embankment. It smashed into two mobile home parks at the edge of the town.

> " *When we got there, there were children hanging on trees.... We had people standing on mobile homes—people trapped. I've never seen anything like this in my life.*
>
> —Jim Pietrangelo, Fort Collins Fire Officer "

Five people drowned in the Fort Collins flash flood. Rescue workers saved over 100 people, though. The water destroyed homes and cars in its path.

What Happens in a Flood?

Floods change people's lives. They can affect their health, their possessions, and their work. Some effects of a flood can be dealt with quickly, but others last a long time.

Immediate health dangers

When a really bad flood suddenly hits a town, people can be swept away by rushing water or by walls of mud washed off the land. They may be injured or drown as they are washed away.

Heavy rains caused this road in Henniker, New Hampshire, to break apart in 2006. About a foot of rain fell over one weekend, causing flooding.

FLOOD FACTS

1. Since 1900, floods have killed more than 10,000 people in the United States alone.

2. It only takes roughly 60 centimeters (2 feet) of water to float a car or even a bus.

3. Most of the people killed by flash floods die because they try to outrun the water, rather than climbing uphill out of its way.

Other hazards

Floating cars, trees, or rocks injure some people. Water can also knock down **powerlines** and break gas and oil pipes. Electricity from the powerlines can **electrocute** anyone touching the water. If broken powerlines touch each other, they produce sparks. These sparks can cause fires in buildings. They can also cause explosions of gas and oil released from broken pipes.

Water, food, and shelter

Even though people are surrounded by flood water, they cannot drink it. The waste in people's drains, called **sewage**, mixes with drinking water in **reservoirs** and wells. This makes the tap water too **polluted** to drink.

People affected by flooding often have no food. Food stores are washed away, polluted, or out of reach in buildings that are completely covered by water or mud. Farm animals may be washed away or drowned and farmers' **crops** may be ruined.

In a flood, people have little shelter. Their homes are sometimes washed away or else full of water.

In 2002 a flood in southern Russia killed around 100 people and made about 100,000 homeless.

Long-term damage

After the rains stop and flood waters drain away, problems may continue. It takes a long time to clean and repair ruined houses, factories, and schools, and to clear streets. During that time, people may have to manage without homes, and places to learn or to earn money. Without **powerlines** and telephone lines, people cannot operate machinery or get in touch with others. If roads, railways, bridges, and vehicles have been washed away or damaged, people cannot travel to work or leave to get food, water, or new clothes.

Polluted water, soggy materials, damp food, and dead animals are just the sort of places that **viruses** and **bacteria** like to live. Viruses and bacteria cause dangerous diseases such as **dysentery**, which spreads when people drink polluted water. People with dysentery lose water through **diarrhea** and sickness and become **dehydrated**. They need to drink clean water to get better, but after a flood drinking water is often polluted—so it makes them even more sick.

When people clear up after floods, they often wear protective clothing. This keeps them safe from diseases or other hazards in the water.

What should people do in a flood?

If a flood happens, keep calm but act quickly to avoid dangers. You and your family or should:

- keep a radio and mobile phone close by so you know what is happening
- alert your neighbors, especially the elderly
- be prepared to move to higher ground
- try to avoid moving at night when you cannot see hazards
- do what the emergency services (such as the police) tell you to do
- keep out of flood water if possible, as it may be hazardous
- if you have to get in the water, use a stick to test the depth of the water
- keep away from power lines and from water near storm drains, as it moves fast
- take pets with you when you move, or put them in a dry place with food. Three out of every ten pet owners risk their lives trying to rescue pets.

Never attempt to wade through floodwater. Wait somewhere safe until emergency service rescue workers come to rescue you.

Who Helps When Floods Happen?

Imagine you wake up one morning to find that your house is flooded with dirty water. Who will help?

The first people to arrive on the scene are workers from the emergency services. The police, fire, and ambulance services make sure people are safe and treat any minor injuries. Local government and army workers help stop further flooding by making walls of sandbags. They also give out clean drinking water and food.

Emergency services may help people move to a safe place, away from the flood water and any hazards caused by flooding. This is called **evacuation**. Rescue workers may use boats, helicopters, and even divers to evacuate people.

Rescue workers use buildings such as gymnasiums as temporary shelters for flood victims. They bring in supplies of drinking water and food, dry clothes and blankets, and sometimes heaters.

Helping out

Poor people who live in poor countries may have to rely more on outside help when disaster strikes. Many local people may want to help but do not have the money to buy medicines and food. They do not usually have the equipment to help rescue people or give them shelter.

After bad floods, other countries and **charities** such as the Red Cross help by sending **aid**. Aid includes useful basic things such as dry food, plastic sheeting, and other materials to make shelters. It also includes pumps to remove water from buildings and medicines such as special drinks to prevent **dehydration**. Aid might also involve helping flood victims plan how to cope better with future floods.

Rice is distributed to flood victims in the Terai region of Nepal in 2008.

Helping get back to normal

Once the flood waters have drained away, different help is needed to get life back to normal. This can take a very long time.

The first step is to see how much damage has been caused. Local governments hire engineers (machine experts) and builders to test the safety of damaged buildings, bridges, and roads. They decide whether they can be repaired or if they need to be rebuilt. Plumbers and electricians test and mend water pipes and **power lines**. **Insurance** agents work out how much it will cost to replace damaged things.

Possessions and household objects that were covered with **polluted** water usually need to be destroyed. This includes not only photos, books, and TVs, but also carpets, sofas, and cushions. When the house is empty, it can be bleached all over to clean it. It then has to dry out. Each half inch thickness of house brick takes a week to dry out.

It can take a long time for people to clear up. They have to shovel mud out of their homes or remove water with buckets or pumps.

United Kingdom, 2007

Throughout the months of June and July in 2007, severe flooding plagued several areas in the United Kingdom. Record rainfall caused several rivers to burst their banks, flooding streets, businesses, and homes. Tens of thousands of people were forced to **evacuate**. The summer floods were responsible for 13 deaths.

According to Britain's Environment Agency, a total of 56,000 homes and businesses were flooded that summer. In areas, the water was 2 meters (6 feet) deep. The flooding also cut off water supplies to hundreds of thousands of people for weeks.

> " *I'm having trouble getting to water as I don't drive and have three small children and I can't get to supermarkets to get bottled water.*
>
> —Samantha, flood victim from Gloucester, England "

NORTH YORKSHIRE

Scarborough

Old Malton
• Norton

York

This photo shows flooding in the village of Upton upon Severn, England, in July 2007. The flooding is a result of 120 millimeters (4.7 inches) falling very quickly.

Can Floods Be Predicted?

Floods cause so much devastation that people work very hard to predict when they might happen. They try to discover when and how bad weather will affect particular areas of land.

Weather

Forecasting or predicting weather accurately is not easy, but modern equipment helps. **Scientists** use **satellites** to take pictures of clouds above Earth. The photos show how big the clouds are and how fast they are moving. The scientists use sensitive **radars** that can detect how much rain or snow there is in the air. They also observe rain clouds and waves at sea from planes or helicopters.

People who work at weather stations collect even more information. They measure the amount of rain that falls each day, how fast snow and ice are melting, and how hot the air is. They record how fast the wind is blowing and how much water is in rivers, **reservoirs**, and lakes.

This photograph was taken from a satellite. It shows a spiral of clouds bringing wet weather to the land beneath.

Knowing the land

Bad weather will only cause a flood if the land cannot drain away the water quickly enough. Areas on tops of hills or with thick **topsoil** are less likely to flood than areas by a river or on hard rock. People record information, such as how hilly the land is and how near it is to the sea or rivers. They store information in computers and use it to make maps showing land that may flood in the future.

Flood risk

When heavy rains arrive, scientists look at how high rivers are and weather forecasts to see how much more rain is expected. Then, using maps of the land and records of floods in the past, they warn people who are in areas at risk from flooding.

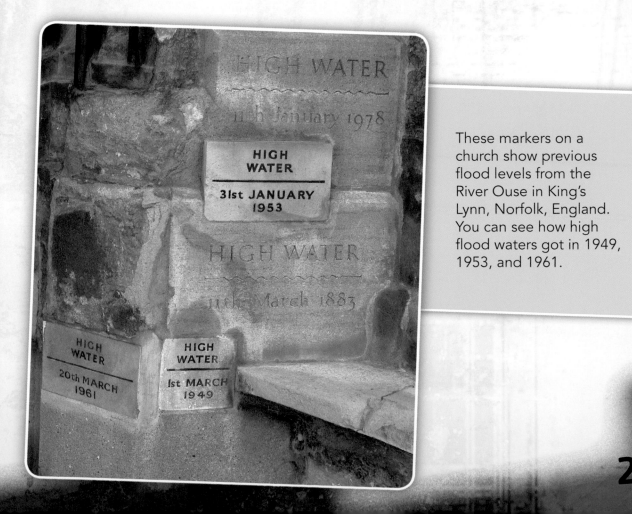

These markers on a church show previous flood levels from the River Ouse in King's Lynn, Norfolk, England. You can see how high flood waters got in 1949, 1953, and 1961.

How Do People Prevent Floods?

In areas where floods can be predicted, people use different ways to try to prevent or reduce them. People control the amount of water in rivers by building **dams** and **flood barriers**. Large amounts of water that might cause flooding are then stored in **reservoirs**. People make the sides of rivers higher by building walls called **levees**. This helps stop rivers from overflowing. They also dig drainage channels, so if rivers do overflow, the water drains away more easily. In coastal areas, people build sea walls to help keep waves off land.

Water runs faster off land where there is little **topsoil** to soak it up. In these places, people plant trees on hillsides around rivers and streams. These help stop topsoil **erosion**—when the soil is washed, blown, or rubbed away. This slows down the flow of water toward **floodplains**.

The Thames flood barrier was built to prevent floods in London. It stops high sea **tides** from moving up the Thames River.

Building to control floods

In floodplains, floods often cannot be prevented, so people build villages, towns, and cities with the effects of flooding in mind. Houses are sometimes built on pillars or stilts so the owners can live above the flood waters. Houses are also built with materials that are not ruined by flood water, such as tiled concrete floors instead of wooden ones. **Power lines** and electrical sockets are positioned high on walls, and drainpipes can be blocked to stop **polluted** water from **sewage** pipes entering the house.

Sometimes houses are designed to keep water out. People may build watertight brick walls around houses or wells. They may also fit special slots around doors and windows. When flood waters rise, they fix floodboards—watertight doors—into the slots.

These houses have been built on stilts to protect them from flooding.

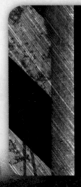

Acting like a sponge
Floodplains soak up large amounts of water like a sponge. The water then drains away slowly. When people build on floodplains, the land soaks up less water, which means floods are more serious.

How do people prepare for floods?

These are some things people need to do or to have if a flood strikes:

- Flood kit: this might include a flashlight or storm lantern, a battery or wind-up radio, a mobile phone, rubber gloves, waterproof boots, or waders, waterproof clothing, a first-aid kit and blankets.

- **Insurance:** this means that damaged or ruined possessions and buildings can be replaced. Details of the insurance should be kept as part of the flood kit.

- Emergency list: this is a list of useful phone numbers such as the emergency services and local flood information. Know who is responsible for doing what during and after a flood.

- Safekeeping: store valuables and important documents such as passports upstairs or in a high and dry place.

A radio, first-aid kit, bottled water, batteries, canned food, and a flashlight are items you might want to pack in your emergency flood kit.

Can everyone prepare for floods?

Poorer people are affected most by flooding. They cannot afford to build houses or roads that can survive floods. They cannot afford to buy insurance that would pay to rebuild their houses quickly if they are damaged by floods. They may live in countries that do not have the resources to predict floods accurately. They may not have radios, TVs, or telephones, which would alert them to a flood risk.

FLOOD FACTS

Governments in different countries have standard ways of telling their people how bad floods are.

1 "Flood Watch" is the least serious. It means flooding is possible, so be aware of water levels and change travel plans.

2 "Severe Flood Warning" is the most serious. It means severe flooding is now expected. People should be prepared to lose power supplies and do as the emergency services tell them if they have to **evacuate** their homes.

These houses in the Philippines have been severely damaged by flooding because they were not very strong. Their owners may be too poor to rebuild them any better.

25

Bangladesh

Bangladesh is a country in Asia where over 150 million people live. It is at the **delta** of three major rivers—the Ganges, Brahmaputra, and Meghna. Each year during the **monsoon**, normal flooding affects one-third of the country.

> 66 *People in the rural areas know how to live with flooding, as they have learned from their **ancestors**. My straw and bamboo house would not be able to withstand the rush of flood water, so it can be taken apart and loaded onto my boat.*
>
> —Matbar Samad, from a village near Dhaka 99

Groups of villagers meet to discuss their flood plans before the monsoon season. They prepare by building walls around wells and **levees** along rivers. Families make and store medicines that treat the illnesses caused by flooding. They often keep ducks for fresh meat and eggs because ducks can swim. If they keep chickens—which cannot swim—they are put in cages that can float!

Bangladeshi children are taught how to use boats so they can use them during floods.

Disaster

Sometimes particularly bad floods happen in Bangladesh. In 1998 heavy monsoon rains and unusually high **tides** flooded over two-thirds of the country for nine weeks. Thirty million people were affected. Around 1,000 people were drowned, **electrocuted**, or bitten by poisonous snakes in the water.

Over the following months, many more people suffered as diseases such as **dysentery** spread. Food and drinking water became scarce.

Local flood planning could not cope. One flood shelter had just three toilets for 2,000 people. Ruined roads, bridges, and railroads meant villages were cut off. Other countries and organizations helped by sending **aid**, including steel bridges and sacks of wheat. After the floods, the country invested in building thousands of miles of new levees. But this may just mean that future floods will affect different areas.

This passenger train derailed into flood waters, killing at least 50 people in Nalgonda, India, in October 2005.

What About Floods in the Future?

Scientists are noticing changes in the world's **climate**. Some of this is just the natural difference that happens from year to year. Some is likely to be the result of global warming. This is when **pollution** in the atmosphere helps to increase the temperature on Earth. Global warming is causing ice at the **poles** to melt. This will cause a rise in **sea levels**. Global warming is also **evaporating** more water from the oceans, which may result in heavier storms that cause more floods.

Serious floods have always been part of life on Earth but they seem to be on the increase. We can all make an effort to learn how our activities affect climate and influence natural disasters such as flooding. We are becoming better at predicting floods. We must also make sure that more people—rich and poor—are prepared when flood waters rise. With careful planning, we can help make the floods of the future less damaging. This will allow life to return to normal more quickly after disaster strikes.

Ten million people across the world are at constant risk of coastal flooding.

Major Floods of Recent Times

Bangladesh, 1970
Heavy rains during a big cyclone caused floods that killed up to 500,000 people and left millions more homeless.

Zhejiang province, China, 1991
Taihu Lake, at the mouth of the Yangtze River in China, flooded in 1991, covering an important industrial and agricultural region. Over 2,000 people died and a million homes were swept away. Overall, the flood affected the lives of 220 million people.

Mississippi, 1993
Over 70,000 people were made homeless after floods in 1993 in Mississippi. Nearly 50,000 homes were damaged or destroyed, and 52 people died. Over 30,000 square kilometers (18,641 square miles) of farmland with **crops** and farm animals were ruined. Damage was estimated at between 15 and 20 billion dollars.

Poland and Germany, 1997
In 1997 the River Oder burst its banks, affecting over 1,000 cities, towns, and villages in Poland. Over 50 people died.

Mozambique, 2002
After a **tropical** storm, two years' worth of rain fell in two weeks, leaving half a million people homeless. More than 700 people died and hundreds of thousands relied on food **aid**.

Central Europe, 2002
In 2002 heavy August rainfall swelled the rivers Danube in Hungary, the Elbe in Germany, and the Vlatva in the Czech Republic to their highest levels for a century. Tens of thousands of people had to **evacuate** their homes in Prague, Budapest, and Dresden. Damage costs were around $20 billion.

Mongolia, 2009
The worst flooding in over 40 years killed at least 24 people in July of 2009. Heavy rains caused flash floods around the capital city of Ulan Bator, damaging and destroying homes, leaving thousands of people homeless.

Glossary

aid help given as money, medicine, food, or other essential items

ancestor relative in the past such as a great-great-grandparent

bacteria small living things that can cause diseases

charities groups that collect money and give out aid

climate usual weather patterns for an area

crops plants that are grown to eat

dam barrier built across a river to stop its normal flow. Dams are also used to store water in a reservoir.

dehydrated (dehydration) without enough water

delta triangular area of land where slow-moving river water meets the sea

diarrhea when illness makes a person's feces like liquid. Diarrhea can be very serious if not treated properly.

dysentery disease of the stomach caused by bacteria. Dysentery causes severe diarrhea and dehydration.

electrocute kill by electric shock

embankment raised road or railway

erosion wearing away by wind, water, or rubbing

evacuate (evacuation) remove people from a dangerous place until it is safe

evaporate (evaporating) when something turns from liquid to gas

fertile describes soil that produces lots of crops

flood barrier structure to control the flow of water in a river

floodplain area of land that normally floods after heavy rainfall

groundwater water found in soil or in cracks in rocks

insurance payments of small regular amounts of money to an insurance company, to make sure repairs to damage after an accident or disaster such as a flood can be paid for

levees raised walls or banks at the edge of a river

monsoon wet season in parts of Asia, Africa, and elsewhere

nutrients chemicals that are needed for growth and development

poles the north pole and the south pole—the most northerly and southerly places on Earth. They are covered in thick ice.

polluted (pollution) when something is spoiled and made unhealthy by something else

power line main cable that carries electricity

radar special machine that uses invisible rays to detect where things are

reservoir large natural or man-made lake used to store water

satellite object that goes around the Earth in space. Satellites do jobs such as sending out TV signals or taking photographs.

scientist person who studies aspects of the world around us

sea level level of the sea surface

sewage waste matter from toilets and drains carried in sewers

temperate climate that is warm and dry in summer and wet and mild in winter

tide regular rise and fall of the sea

topsoil upper fertile layer of soil. Topsoil soaks up groundwater.

tropical from the tropics, an area near the equator that is hot all year round

virus tiny chemical substances that can cause diseases

Find out more

Books

Allen, Tony. *Wild Water: Floods*. (Chicago: Raintree, 2005).

Fine, Jil. *Floods*. (New York: Children's Press, 2006).

Winget, Mary. *Floods*. (Minneapolis, Minn.: Lerner, 2008).

Woods, Michael, and Mary B. Woods. *Floods*. (Minneapolis, Minn.: Lerner, 2007).

Websites

FEMA for Kids

www.fema.gov/kids/floods

The website of the Federal Emergency Management Agency, with useful advice about what to do in a flood.

The Hows and Whys of Floods

www.pbs.org/newshour/infocus/floods/science.html

A website about floods from PBS.

Weather Wiz Kids

www.weatherwizkids.com/weather-rain.htm

This website contains lots of information about weather and floods.

Index